MARIE CHAN *Illustrated by* SIAN JAMES

MAMIE
TAKES A STAND

TEN PEAKS PRESS®
EUGENE, OR

Acknowledgments

I am grateful for Linda Doler and Mitchell Kim, members of the Tape family who graciously gave their time for interviews and shared their historic family photos to help inform my research for this book. I appreciate Alisa J. Kim's insights on the historic significance of this case and her help as the initial contact. The legacy of the Tape family lives on in these pages.

Scripture quotations are taken from the Holy Bible, New International Version®, NIV®. Copyright © 1973, 1978, 1984, 2011 by Biblica, Inc.® Used by permission of Zondervan. All rights reserved worldwide. www.zondervan.com. The "NIV" and "New International Version" are trademarks registered in the United States Patent and Trademark Office by Biblica, Inc.®

Published in association with Embolden Media Group, www.emboldenmediagroup.com

Cover design by Connie Gabbert Design + Illustration
Interior design by Nicole Dougherty; Interior images © tjhunt, subjug / Getty Images
Photo of Sian James by Naomi Wilde Photography
Photos on pages 42-43 used with permission. Page 42, left: by William Shew, Linda Doler collection. Page 42, center: by Charles Lake Cramer, Linda Doler collection. Page 42, right: "Mamie Hunter Lowe, photo," ca. 1940; Case file 12016/8690 for Gertrude E. Chan, Box 10; Series: Case Files of Investigations Not Resulting in Warrant Proceedings; Immigration and Naturalization Service, RG 85; National Archives at San Francisco. Page 43, left: 7360 Chinese Public School Children, San Francisco, Cal. Taber Photo, San Francisco, Cal., Roy D. Graves pictorial collection, BANC PIC 1905.17500 v.29:119--ALB, The Bancroft Library, University of California, Berkeley. Page 43, right: Alisa J. Kim collection.

For bulk or special sales, please call 1-800-547-8979. Email: CustomerService@hhpbooks.com

 TEN PEAKS PRESS is a federally registered trademark of the Hawkins Children's LLC. Harvest House Publishers, Inc., is the exclusive licensee of this trademark.

Mamie Takes a Stand
Copyright © 2024 by Marie Chan. Artwork copyright © 2024 by Sian James
Published by Ten Peaks Press, an imprint of Harvest House Publishers
Eugene, Oregon 97408

ISBN 978-0-7369-8732-5 (hardcover)

Library of Congress Control Number: 2023936207

Printed in China

24 25 26 27 28 29 30 31 / LP / 10 9 8 7 6 5 4 3 2 1

This book is dedicated to God,
who created each person with dignity and worth.
And to children everywhere—may you know
you are loved and valued in God's sight.

Mamie Hunter Tape was born in the heart of Gold Mountain* and searched for a treasure greater than gold. She found hints of it shining in her mother's handmade porcelain dishes and paintings of shimmering flowers and landscapes. She discovered glimmers of it in numbers and letters when she learned to read.

*Chinese name for San Francisco, *Gum Saan* or *jīn shān* (金山)

Mamie wanted more. She wanted to go to school with the children in her neighborhood.

But in 1884, Chinese children were not allowed to attend San Francisco public schools.

Mamie's parents—Joseph and Mary Tape—had immigrated from China to California. Mamie was the first in her family to be born in America.

From her earliest baby steps, Mamie played with
the children in her neighborhood. She spoke English
and wore American clothes like they did. Her white
friends went to Spring Valley School, right around
the corner, so Mamie hoped she could go there too.

In September, Mamie dressed in clothes
as crisp and clean as a fresh fall day.
She was excited about her first day of school!

What would she learn?
Would the lessons be hard or easy?
Would her teacher be nice?

Mamie would be the first in her family to go to
an American public school. Her parents hoped
her little brother, Frank, would join her soon.
Her sister Emily was too young to go to school.

Mamie and her mother walked one block from their home on Green Street to enter Spring Valley School.

But the principal, Miss Hurley, blocked the way.

Because Mamie was Chinese.

America was Mamie's home.
Why didn't her own country welcome her?
Why did she feel like a foreigner in her homeland?
She had done nothing wrong.

As Mamie turned toward home, she peered
through the window and looked longingly
at her friends studying at their desks.

An open mind opened doors.

Now that door slammed shut in her face
like a locked treasure chest.

Would Mamie ever find the key to unlock it?

Her parents asked the school superintendent many times to admit Mamie, but the response was always the same—NO.

Mamie's parents believed that all people were born with the right to learn, for God had made them all. Mamie's family decided to stand up and fight for their rights.

First, Mamie's dad asked for help from Frederick Bee, a respected lawyer. Mr. Bee had represented Chinese people when mobs had burned down their homes and shops.

Mr. Bee wrote a letter to the school board, saying Mamie had the right to go to Spring Valley School because she was a citizen, born in the United States.

School and state officials replied, claiming that the Chinese were "dangerous to the well-being of the state."

Eight-year-old Mamie was young, healthy, and kind. How could she be dangerous?

The Tapes made headlines while
the school board argued about Mamie.

The school board voted to fire teachers and
principals if they admitted Chinese children.

Closed minds closed doors.

"I'd rather go to jail
than allow a Chinese
child to be admitted
to the schools."

Mamie heard how heartbroken her parents
were at the school board's response.

Mamie knew she was an American.
The school board misjudged her because of her race
and her Chinese face. They judged her as if all they
saw was her Chinese name, 遠香, *Yuen Heung,*
meaning "the fragrance of a distant land."

In fact, Mamie didn't play with Chinese children because none of them lived nearby.

Mamie only saw a few Chinese people—workers in the fields near the marina. She giggled whenever they surprised her family with tasty jade-green *bok choy* and *gai choy* next to their gate.

Mamie enjoyed eating both Chinese and American food: *chow mein*, rice, and corn on the cob. Why couldn't she be both Chinese and American?

Mamie admired her dad's determination not to give up the fight. Next, her dad asked another lawyer, William Gibson, to represent Mamie in court. Mr. Gibson's family understood Chinese culture and helped Chinese people in need.

William's father, Reverend Otis Gibson, had preached
boldly to persuade others to stop hurting the Chinese:
"The doors of our country are open equally. . .
We have room for all."

Mr. Gibson wanted the Tapes' fight to open doors not
only for Mamie but for all Chinese American children.

Mamie didn't like hearing the school leaders call Chinese people mean names. She knew they acted unfairly out of fear and prejudice. If the school board let Mamie in, then they would have to let all the Chinese children go to the public schools.

Despite the bigger battle ahead,
Mamie lifted her chin and focused her
gaze on stepping closer to her treasure.
She would stand tall.

Four months later, in January 1885, a judge ruled that state law and the Fourteenth Amendment to the US Constitution gave Mamie the right to a free public education. This amendment stated that being born in America gave Mamie all the rights of a citizen. Mamie could not be excluded from Spring Valley School because her parents were Chinese.

Unhappy with the outcome, the school board took the case to a higher court.

But the Tape family stood firm like redwood trees,
ready to face the storm that tried to destroy the
dreams of immigrant families.

As the lawyers argued their cases before the judges,
Mamie watched her friends walk to school in the mornings
without her. In the afternoons, she listened to their chatter.
What gems of wisdom had they learned that she had missed?

Finally, on March 3, 1885, the California Supreme Court reaffirmed that public schools should be open to all children and that Mamie had the right to go to school, regardless of her race. The court ordered Miss Hurley to let Mamie go to Spring Valley School. The Tapes had won their case!

Mamie prepared again to enter Spring Valley School—this time with lawyers by her side.

Surely Miss Hurley couldn't stop her now.

But Miss Hurley had a new list of excuses for not admitting Mamie.

Excuse #1: No vaccination certificate.
The next day Mamie brought one.

Excuse #2: No room in her grade.
Mamie could be put on the waiting list.

How much longer would she have to wait? The school year was almost over!

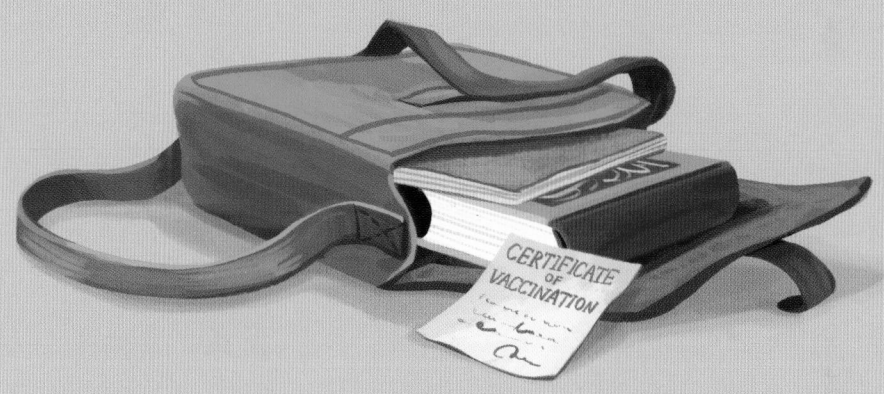

The excuses only covered up the school's real reason for not letting Mamie in—racism.

The school superintendent didn't want Chinese students mixing with white students. He feared that white students would leave once Chinese students came. He urged the state to quickly pass a new law to make separate Chinese schools. Now Mamie could only go to a segregated public school, far from where she lived.

Outraged, Mamie's mother would not stay silent. She wrote a letter to the school board to protest their unfair treatment of Mamie. Her letter was printed in the newspaper.

Daily Alta California

SAN FRANCISCO: THURSDAY, APRIL 16, 1885.

BOARD OF EDUCATION

CHINESE MOTHER'S LETTER

A LETTER FROM MRS. TAPE

The following is a verbatim copy of a letter received from Mrs. Tape, in regard to her children at present attending the Chinese school:

SAN FRANCISCO, April 8, 1885

To the Board of Education— DEAR SIRS: I see that you are going to make all sorts of excuses to keep my child out off the Public schools. Dear sirs, Will you please to tell me! Is it a disgrace to be Born a Chinese? Didn't God make us all!!! What right! have you to bar my children out of the school because she is a chinese Decend. . . It seems no matter how a Chinese may live and dress so long as you know they Chinese, Then they are hated as one. There is not any right or justice for them. . . I will let the world see sir What justice there is When it is govern by the Race prejudice men!

. . . Mrs. M. Tape.

Although the Tape family was against segregation, Mamie was the first girl to attend the Chinese Primary School when it opened on April 13, 1885. Her younger brother, Frank, went, too, and wore a suit. Mamie put a stylish straw hat over her braided hair and ribbon. She straightened her pink stockings and buttoned her boots. Then the two set off for their first day of school.

Mamie rode in her father's wagon. The horse's hooves clip-clopped against the cobblestone roads. The breeze from the bay blew against her face.

Ding, ding, rang the cable cars as they glided up and down the hill. Mamie remembered when the city had built the cable car tracks. Just like the tracks made deep grooves in the street, she, too, would carve a new path to fulfill her dream of a better education.

The hustle and bustle of Chinatown was much
louder than Mamie's quiet neighborhood of Cow Hollow.
The scent of garlic, ginger, fish, and herbs filled the air.

Mamie climbed the stairs to get to her classroom above a grocery store. She counted the numbers posted on the wall. Seventeen wooden desks were lined up in neat rows.

Mamie and Frank stood out from the other Chinese students who lived in Chinatown and wore traditional Chinese clothes. Some of the boys were twice her brother's age, but they all learned together in the same classroom with one young teacher, Miss Thayer.

Mamie turned the pages of *McGuffey's Second Reader*.
She studied stories about bubbles and birds, dolls and dogs.
She read poems like "Twinkle, Twinkle, Little Star."

Mamie even brought her roller skates
and zoomed around during recess.

In those days, few Chinese girls were encouraged to go to school, so Mamie was often the only girl in her class. But that didn't stop her from using her sharp mind and learning as much as she could until she completed all the grades at the school.

Mamie would not let racism steal her treasure—her rights as a citizen and her right to a public education. She broke new ground and staked her claim to truth and justice. The court battle had refined her like gold from the mines of Gold Mountain.

Mamie lived out the true meaning of her Chinese name, 遠香, *Yuen Heung*, "distant fragrance," as her victory in court reached beyond the borders of San Francisco and opened the door for all Chinese children in California to have a free public education.

In years to come, many families and many brave girls,
like Ruby Bridges, Linda Brown, and Sylvia Mendez,
would also fight for the right to go to integrated schools.
They chiseled and hammered away at the mountain
of exclusion to create a new path toward unity.
They discovered the power of knowledge and
belonging buried deep below boulders of injustice.

Mamie found a treasure worth more than gold when she lived to see her younger sisters, children, grandchildren, and great-grandchildren go to integrated schools. Her courage paved the way for schools to become places where children would not be judged by their race or ancestry, but would be welcomed and given an equal opportunity to learn.

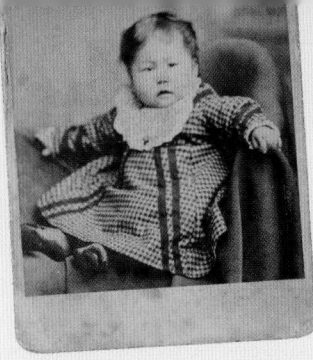

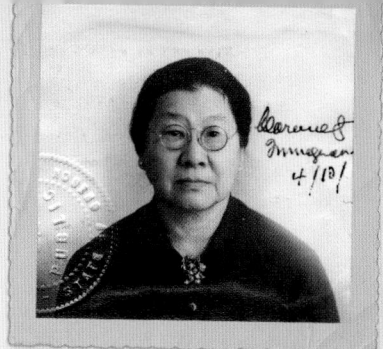

One-year-old Mamie Tape, c. 1877.
Courtesy of Linda Doler.

Mamie Tape in her teens.
Courtesy of Linda Doler.

Mamie Hunter [Tape] Lowe, c. 1940.
Courtesy of National Archives–San Francisco.

Afterword

When Mamie was older, she became friends with Chinese girls and women who lived at the mission led by Donaldina Cameron and her assistant, Tien Fuh Wu, in San Francisco's Chinatown. Mamie valued caring for immigrants in need.

Today the Chinese Primary School is named Gordon Lau Elementary School, after San Francisco's first Chinese American supervisor, who fought for civil rights. The diverse staff at Spring Valley School now welcomes children of all races, celebrates their ethnic heritage, and is committed to the success of all students.

Author's Note About the Research

I have made every effort to make Mamie's story as accurate as possible and have used mostly primary sources for my research. I am thankful for archivists, historians, professors, and members of the Tape family, whom I interviewed, for their help in piecing together Mamie's story. However, unlike Ruby Bridges and Sylvia Mendez, who are highlighted in more contemporary cases of school integration, Mamie was not interviewed by the press at that time, nor did she often speak publicly about the case or write articles and books about her experience. Mamie thought additional court records may have been destroyed in the 1906 San Francisco fire and earthquake. Furthermore, deciphering the accuracy of some sources was difficult because they seemed biased and may have been used as anti-Chinese propaganda during the time of the 1882 Chinese Exclusion Act.

Chinese American historians Him Mark Lai and Philip Choy conducted a rare interview of Mamie in her nineties, right before she passed away, but Mamie gave only a few details about her experience and role in the court case. Immigration interviews of Tape family members and Mamie's neighbor that I obtained from the National Archives gave more clues as to what happened during the time of the *Tape v. Hurley* case, but they don't reveal much about how Mamie felt.

I interviewed Mamie Tape's great-granddaughter, Linda Doler, who said that Mamie did not leave any journals. Therefore, I based some of my biography on how her great-granddaughter remembered Mamie as a person and on archival and family photographs. During my research of this hidden figure, I realized how much the voices of people of color have been silenced in this country due to limited documentation of their experiences. It is important to amplify their stories so future generations may learn this valuable history.

Historic Note

Mamie's victory in *Tape v. Hurley* was an important first step that affirmed the rights of citizenship and a public education for children born in the United States of Chinese parents—rights protected by the Fourteenth Amendment of the US Constitution. Racism is complex. Mamie won her case—both in the California Superior Court and, when the school board appealed, in the California Supreme Court—but full implementation of integration did not come until decades later. Mamie set the precedent for future cases in the fight for equality in education.

Finally, in 1947, Sylvia Mendez, along with the Estrada, Guzman, Palomino, and Ramirez families, who represented four Orange County school districts, won their case in *Mendez et al. v. Westminster et al.* This ruling allowed children of Mexican descent to attend their local public schools instead of separate Mexican schools. Soon afterward, California banned segregation of all public schools.

Subsequently, the US Supreme Court ruled that separate schools were "inherently unequal" in *Brown et al. v. Board of Education of Topeka et al.* Despite this court victory in 1954, the year Ruby Bridges was born, the enforcement of this new law did not occur in New Orleans, Louisiana, until Ruby was six years old. Ruby still faced terrible opposition when she bravely integrated William Frantz Elementary School as the first African American student in 1960.

Trailblazers in the fight for civil rights sacrificed and took a bold stance. They often did not personally experience the fulfillment of their dreams but only envisioned them from afar. As the author of Hebrews wrote, "Now faith is confidence in what we hope for and assurance about what we do not see" (Hebrews 11:1).

May we continue to learn from these courageous examples and press on until "justice roll[s] on like a river, righteousness like a never-failing stream!" (Amos 5:24).

"Chinese Public School Children, San Francisco, Cal."
Photo by Isaiah Taber. Courtesy of Bancroft Library, UC Berkeley.

The Tape Family, c. 1884-1885. Courtesy of Alisa J. Kim.

Timeline

1849	Large groups of Chinese immigrants arrived in San Francisco ("Gold Mountain") to mine for gold during the California Gold Rush.
1865	The Civil War ended.
1868	The Burlingame Treaty was signed between the US and China to allow free migration between the two countries. The Fourteenth Amendment was passed.
1869	Chinese workers helped complete the transcontinental railroad.
1876	Mamie Tape was born in San Francisco, California.
1882	The Chinese Exclusion Act was passed to restrict Chinese workers from coming to the US.
1884	In September, Mamie Tape was excluded from Spring Valley Primary School. Look Tin Sing won his case for US citizenship.
1885	In January, the California Superior Court ruled in Mamie's favor in *Tape v. Hurley*. The San Francisco Board of Education appealed.
1885	In March, the California Supreme Court affirmed Mamie's right to go to school. Assembly Bill 268 was passed to establish separate schools for Chinese children.
1885	In April, Mamie entered the Chinese Primary School in Chinatown.
1885	In August, Mamie's mother, Mary Tape, displayed her artwork at the Industrial Exhibition of the Mechanics' Institute, a library and cultural center in San Francisco, where she took classes and received her diploma in ceramic arts.
1892	Mary Tape was featured in a newspaper article for her excellence in photography. A journalist wrote that Mamie played the piano well, especially popular American songs. He was impressed with the similarities between the Tape family and other American families.
1895	The Tape family moved to Berkeley.
1897	Mamie married Herman Lowe.
1898	In *United States v. Wong Kim Ark*, the US Supreme Court affirmed the citizenship of all who were born in the United States, including children of immigrants.

CALIFORNIA SUPERIOR COURT

CALIFORNIA SUPREME COURT

1898	Mamie's son, Harold, was born.
1901	Mamie's daughter, Emily Gertrude, was born. She was named after Mamie's two sisters.
1906	The San Francisco earthquake destroyed much of Chinatown. Spring Valley Primary School was rebuilt in a different location. The Chinese Primary School was renamed the "Oriental School" to exclude more Asian students from white public schools.
1924	Nine-year-old Martha Lum was not allowed to attend her local Mississippi public school because of her Chinese ancestry. Her case, *Gong Lum et al. v. Rice et al.*, went to the US Supreme Court in 1927.
1941	Japanese planes attacked Pearl Harbor.
1943	The Magnuson Act, passed on December 17, repealed the Chinese Exclusion Act because China became allies with the United States during World War II.
1947	In *Mendez et al. v. Westminster et al.*, five families from Westminster, Garden Grove, El Modena, and Santa Ana, California, won their school integration case.
1954	In *Brown et al. v. Board of Education et al.*, the US Supreme Court ruled that separate schools were not equal and that segregated schools were against the law.
1960	Ruby Bridges became the first African American student at William Frantz Elementary School in New Orleans.
1972	Mamie Tape Lowe died.
1977	Lonnie Chin, a Chinese American teacher, became principal of Spring Valley School.
1995	Mary Tape's art was exhibited in "With New Eyes: Toward an Asian American Art History in the West" at the San Francisco State University Gallery. The Tape descendants were reunited to celebrate the exhibit.
1998	The Chinese Primary School (later called the "Oriental School") was renamed Gordon J. Lau Elementary School.
2000	Renowned filmmaker Loni Ding made a documentary about Mamie Tape.
2009	The California State Assembly established December 17 as the "Day of Inclusion" to commemorate the repeal of the Chinese Exclusion Act.
2020	PBS premiered the film series *Asian Americans* and featured the *Tape v. Hurley* case in the fight for civil rights.

Discussion Questions

Before Reading

1. Why do you think a Chinese American girl would have to fight for the right to go to school?

2. Have you ever felt excluded? How did you feel? What did you do?

During Reading

1. Why didn't Miss Hurley think Mamie was an American citizen? What makes someone an American?

2. If you were Mamie Tape, what would you do if you were excluded from school?

3. How did the Tape family fight peacefully for their civil rights? *(For example, they wrote letters and hired lawyers.)*

4. What character qualities did Mamie and her family show that inspire you? *(For example, they demonstrated courage, perseverance, and resilience.)*

After Reading

1. In the story, how did Mr. Bee and Mr. Gibson, the two American lawyers, use their skills and knowledge for good? How did the school superintendent and Miss Hurley, the school principal, wrongly use their power to protect their privilege and position? What does it mean to be an advocate for someone else?

2. Have you seen others excluded unfairly? What can you do to stand up for what is right?

3. How can you welcome and help immigrant families that are new to the US?

 # Note on Chinese Pronunciations

In Chinese, your family name is stated first and your personal, given name, consisting of one or two characters, follows it. Mamie's father's Chinese name was "Jeu Dip" (*Zhao Xia*, 趙洽). He changed it to Joseph Tape after he emigrated.

Joseph's family name of "Jeu" in *Hoisan-wa*/Toisanese (sometimes written *"Chew"* or *"Jiu"* in Cantonese) is pronounced *"Zhào"* in Mandarin Chinese. "Jeu" sounds like the American first name "Joe," for "Joseph."

The name "Dip" became "Tape" when Joseph married Mary. "Dip" sounds like the German name "Tape." "Dip" is pronounced *"Xiá"* in Mandarin Chinese.

Mamie's Chinese name was *"Yuen Heung"* (Cantonese romanization) and is pronounced *"Yuǎn Xiāng"* (遠香) in Mandarin Chinese. Her full Chinese name was *Jeu Yuen Heung (Zhao Yuan Xiang)*.

Notes

15 — "Dangerous to the well-being of the state." William T. Welcker, quoted in "The Chinese and the Schools," *Sacramento Daily Union*, October 10, 1884. California Digital Newspaper Collection, Center for Bibliographic Studies and Research, University of California, Riverside, https://cdnc.ucr.edu/?a=d&d=SDU18841010.2.8.

16 — "...rather go to jail than allow..." San Francisco school board member Isidor Danielwitz, quoted in "The School Board," *San Francisco Evening Bulletin*, October 22, 1884.

17 — "...in favor of extending the privileges of the public schools to all native-born children irrespective of race or color." Charles Cleveland, quoted in "Board of Education...Chinese Question Again," *Daily Alta California*, October 22, 1884, https://cdnc.ucr.edu/?a=d&d=DAC18841022.2.23.

19 — "*Bok choy* and *gai choy*." Him Mark Lai and Philip Choy, interview with Mamie Tape Lowe and Emily Lowe Lum, July 29, 1972, Portland, OR. Box 25: 18-19, Him Mark Lai research files, additions, 1834-2009 (bulk 1970-2008), AAS ARC 2010/1, Ethnic Studies Library University of California, Berkeley. Digitized recording courtesy of Mae Ngai.

"*Chow mein*, rice, and corn on the cob." Linda Doler, online interview with author, Marie Chan, California, April 29, 2021.

21 — "The doors of our country are open equally... We have room for all." Otis Gibson, *The Chinese in America* (Cincinnati, OH: Hitchcock & Walden, 1877), 279.

31 — "To the Board of Education—DEAR SIRS: I see that..." Mary Tape, "Chinese Mother's Letter," *Daily Alta California*, April 16, 1885. California Digital Newspaper Collection, Center for Bibliographic Studies and Research, University of California, Riverside, https://cdnc.ucr.edu/?a=d&d=DAC18850416.2.3.

36 — "Twinkle, Twinkle, Little Star." William Holmes McGuffey, *McGuffey's Second Eclectic Reader*, rev. ed. (New York: American Book Company, 1920), 16. Originally published in 1879.

36 — "Roller skates." *San Francisco Evening Bulletin*, April 14, 1885, quoted in Victor Low, *The Unimpressible Race: A Century of Educational Struggle by the Chinese in San Francisco* (San Francisco: East/West Pub. Co., 1982), 72.

39 — "*Yuen Heung*" and "distant fragrance." Interview of Mrs. Herman [Mamie Tape] Lowe, July 7, 1930, Portland, file 5017/562, National Archives and Records Administration at Seattle; cited in Mae Ngai, *The Lucky Ones: One Family and the Extraordinary Invention of Chinese America* (New York: Houghton Mifflin Harcourt, 2010), 25.

43 — "Inherently unequal." Milestone Documents, National Archives, transcript of *Brown v. Board of Education (1954)*, https://www.archives.gov/milestone-documents/brown-v-board-of-education.

44 — Some of the information in this timeline is drawn from Daniella Thompson, "The Tapes of Russell Street," Berkeley Architectural Heritage Association, April 30, 2004, https://berkeleyheritage.com/essays/tape_family.html.

46 — Pronunciations drawn from Mae Ngai, *The Lucky Ones: One Family and the Extraordinary Invention of Chinese America* (New York: Houghton Mifflin Harcourt, 2010).

Important Words to Know

ancestry	civil rights	race
assembly	court	racism
bill	foreigner	school board
California Superior Court	Fourteenth Amendment	segregation
California Supreme Court	immigrant	separate
case	integrated	superintendent
Chinese Exclusion Act	lawyer	transcontinental railroad
citizen	prejudice	US Constitution

About the Author & Artist

Marie Chan shares stories that inspire love for all. Being the daughter of Taiwanese immigrants fueled her passion to write children's books that amplify underrepresented voices, highlight hidden figures in Asian American history, and build cross-cultural awareness. As a former California public school teacher, she holds Mamie Tape's story in her heart because she would not have been allowed to teach or study in California if Mamie had not fought against racial discrimination and won her case. Marie lives in California with her husband, two children with a third in heaven, and her giant rabbit, Sunshine.

Connect with her and learn more at mariechan.com and on Instagram @mariechanbooks.

Sian James' vibrant and imaginative illustrations have appeared in projects for several prominent clients, including HarperCollins and Penguin Random House. She currently resides in Cambridge, England, with her husband, her daughter, and their two affectionate cats, Miso and Mochi.

Connect with her and learn more at sianjamesillustration.com and on Instagram @sianjart.